GOVCON

BILLION DOLLAR PLAYBOOK

Billion Dollar Playbook 72 Websites for
Massive Scaling in The Marketplace

GOVCON
BILLION DOLLAR PLAYBOOK

Billion Dollar Playbook
72 Websites for Massive Scaling
in The Marketplace

Eric E. Coffie

www.govcongiants.com

© 2017 Eric E. Coffie
All rights reserved.
ISBN: xxxxxxxxxxxxx
ISBN 13 xxxxxxxxxxxxx
Library of Congress Control Number: 2017910856
CreateSpace Independent Publishing Platform, North Charleston, SC

Billion Dollar Playbook

A THANK YOU TO MY READERS:
YOUR FREE GIFT

I cannot thank you enough for all of the support and encouragement I've received from my colleagues and followers. As a way of expressing my gratitude for purchasing my book, I'm offering a free course exclusively for my readers. In *Government Contracting for Dummies*, you will learn how to get registered to win your first government contract in 90 days or less.

In *Government Contracting for Dummies* you will learn what it means to do federal contracts and how to discover opportunities that exist in the marketplace. After identifying the opportunities in your field of expertise I'll show you exactly where to go to start negotiating the contracts that you choose.

The techniques that I show you will incorporate many of the websites in this resource. Together, we will examine how to use these tools in financially beneficial ways so that you can start engaging clients and customers.

Follow the link below to learn more.

www.freegovconcourse.com

TABLE OF CONTENTS

INTRODUCTION

Searching the web

In a world of Google, Amazon, Apple and YouTube, information is becoming easier to find, catalog, search, and access. But, what happens when you don't know what you're searching for?

What, exactly, happens when there is no directory or website that leads directly to the specific information you are seeking? Sure, you can Google just about anything, but the results are not categorized in an easy to understand manner that takes you from A to Z, from start to finish.

This is the very problem that I encountered when I first took the plunge into the abyss of government contracting. I was inundated with industry veterans (behemoths) that seemed untouchable—yet within a year or so of knocking on doors and following a series of calculated steps, the firms that I represented became the incumbent everyone was gunning for. What first appeared as a cornfield maze that you would brave on Halloween became the yellow brick path to financial stability and success in my business.

Today, I dread the idea of working in the private sector with limited protections and companies intentionally deceiving you. It feels as risky as riding solo through the Wild, Wild West.

Do not be discouraged by the countless agencies, departments, buying methods, documents, forms, and acronyms. The conglomerate firms and daunting government system act as a way of shunning the smaller, often times great firms from entering the marketplace. That's a tragedy considering that small business firms have been the foundation for great wealth in our country for several generations. This does not have to be this way.

In my business it was only after dialing down to specific agencies that the mysteriousness of tackling government contracts went away. Once we learned how to search for the entities that purchased our services, we were able to focus squarely on that target.

In fact, if you look at *USNews'* or *Forbes'* breakdown of the richest counties where residents have the highest median income in the nation, you will find regularly find five of the top 10 wealthiest counties are in the D.C. metro area.

- Loudoun County, Virginia
- Howard County, Maryland
- Fall Church City, Virginia
- Arlington County, Virginia
- Fairfax County, Virginia

WHAT DOES THIS TELL YOU?

Your financial future could be at stake here!

If you are wondering why the process of doing business as a government contractor is "clear as mud," it's because the task of low-wage earners spending trillions annually requires multiple layers of responsibility. Department heads, directors, assistant directors, division directors, and so forth—each layer has a hierarchy which creates its own set of rules.

They may be run independently, but they all must follow the same Federal Acquisition Regulations (FAR).

> *"By failing to prepare, you are preparing to fail"*
> *– Benjamin Franklin*

Throughout this guide, we will teach you how to identify your sweet spot in the market. Contracting officers are always looking for experienced contractors and service providers. The bottom line is: if you can deliver the services at a mutually-agreed price and within a reasonable timeframe, then the government would love to have you as a vendor.

About *Billion-Dollar Playbook*

Let's set the record straight—this is **NOT** a book on how to get, win, or negotiate federal contracts.

This is a book that outlines *where to go* to locate information that will help you determine critical decisions needed to register, identify, negotiate, and win federal contracts.

Here's the good news:

Mostly everything you know about doing business with the U.S. government is free.

Whether you are browsing a website or seeking access to a database, the information is accessible with a few clicks of your mouse.

The only possible speed bump here is that you may be required to register prior to use of certain databases so that the company or organization can cross reference who is requesting government information. But the meat—all of the material itself—is free of charge to view, download, and use.

So if everything is free, what can the problem possibly be?

The problem is that the information is not centralized. There are countless facts and figures spread across a disorganized maze of agencies so what you're looking for can be extremely difficult to come across. To further cloud your research, the common use of acronyms, illogical website descriptions, and a barrage of organizational charts all make it difficult to decipher which websites offer which tools.

This is part of the reason that there is probably one consultant for every 20 registered government contractors. Much like lobbyists are to Congress, consultants are to government contractors. They serve a purpose and offer value due to the disorganization of the system.

Luckily, I've done most of the investigative work needed so that you will be able to get to the right place to find the information you're interested in. I will help you bypass the need to hire a consultant.

It was not until my company had done several million dollars in sales that we elected to hire a consultant. Even after we hired her, it was a waste of profit, as she only referred us to persons that could provide services, but no type of business development.

Prior to hiring our consultant, all of the information we needed to secure our first few dozen contracts was FREE! This step-by-step book helps you avoid the unnecessary work and uncertainty.

We won't tell you how to negotiate, as we suspect that you already know how to handle your own ventures. But, we will help you discover which resources you need to complete contacts with the government, depending on the current status of your federal journey.

By using this book you will save hundreds of hours scouring the internet through old publications, links, articles, and trainings that no longer exist.

As of publication or revision, you have the most UP-TO-DATE information on the market!

Who is Eric Coffie?

My name is Eric Coffie and I have been curious about entrepreneurship and business my entire life.

Since being introduced to the world of government contracting in 2007, I have been fascinated with the endless possibilities surrounding this marketplace. I have watched people secure their financial freedom through federal contracts. This has pushed me to do the same.

With endless opportunities and an open playing field, I thought to myself, "This has got to be the world's best kept secret." A marketplace where people give you the tools, resources, counselors, sometimes contracts—it reminded me of what people think when they are leaving their countries and coming to the United States to pursue the American Dream. It was a dream come true in every sense of the word.

I can personally attest to aiding in the creation of wealth of several families and watching others grow into the seven- and eight-figure arena.

I am currently building my family's wealth in this arena and you can do the same. My goal is to guide you through a marketplace that rewards handsomely for companies that bring value.

For more from the author visit www.govcongiants.com or you can look up his popular YouTube channel Govcon Giants.

My Promise to You

My promise is that you will receive the most current information available at the time of publishing this book. Ninety percent of the websites that you will ever need throughout your journey are printed inside the pages of this hand guide. I am going to tell you exactly where to go for the information and how to use the site.

- ***Why are some government websites not listed in this book?*** The idea behind the book was not to list every single website affiliated with government contracts. The idea was to list the ones I found to be most beneficial for growing a government contracting business. For our purposes, I wanted to focus primarily on the task of winning contracts.

- ***Now let's take it one step further.*** If you fully understand how to navigate and manipulate these sites to the fullest extent possible, you will achieve a degree of expertise far greater than that of the people whom you're serving. In my experience most people only know the knowledge related to doing their specific job; their education stops when their day stops. So you'll be way ahead of the curve in your quest to successful contracting.

A Final Word

Keep in mind that there are literally hundreds of topics we could write about over the course of thousands of pages regarding federal contracting. However, for the purposes of keeping things simple, we have limited the book contents to only the most valuable websites for your benefit.

Additionally, with some of the more commonly used webpages, we have added **quick tips** on alternative methods for using the sites by experienced federal contractors. They are gathering critical market research and performing data mining using the same websites.

Who Should Read the Book?

- If you have tried your hand at government contracting with little or no success – we can help!

- If you are not a prime contractor – we can help!

- If your business is experiencing little or no growth at the time – we can help!

Newbies: You will learn incredible insights into a foreign world and will be able to kick start your career/business in the world of federal contracting.

Experienced Contractors: Use this book as a means of teaching new staff in the office the arithmetic of federal contracting.

Everyone has the opportunity to benefit from the information detailed throughout these pages. Take heed of the resources available to streamline your success!

REGISTRATION SITES

The first step to working for any government entity is to get registered. Before you can work with the federal government, you must become a corporation and apply for your state tax identification number.

1. North America Industry Classification System (NAICS)

It is imperative that you know the NAICS code for the product/service that you will be providing to the government. This is a six-digit code that is used by federal statistical agencies to classify business establishments. Simply put, that is how they track government spending.

Whenever you search for or discuss contract opportunities, the possibilities are typically listed using NAICS codes. As a small business, this code will be used on all of your marketing material to designate your business segment to government officials.

On the NAICS website you have the ability to perform a generic search for your industry. After conducting this search, a list of common keywords will pop up displaying more specific categories. If you click on a given category, you will find a detailed description of the activities associated with that code.

From the keyword search, continue drilling down until you identify your particular niche market. If your business performs multiple services, write down all of the NAICS codes that apply to your business. When you register as a vendor you will only be allowed to choose one primary NAICS code for your business.

FYI: When registering as a government vendor you are permitted to have more than one NAICS code. However, whichever you list as your primary code will be your maximum ceiling for receiving small business contracts.

Website: https://www.census.gov/eos/www/naics/

Pro Tip: Primary NAICS

- **Identify all potential NAICS codes (everything your business does)**

- **Compare NAICS codes against the size standards chart to see which code has the highest $ or employee threshold.**

- **When you register to be a vendor, make sure that the NAICS code with the highest threshold is the primary one you use**

---

2. Dun and Bradstreet, DUNS Numbers

When building a business, the first thing you will do is set up your corporation. After putting that in place, you will apply online with the IRS for your Employer Identification Number (EIN). The EIN is the Social Security number, so to speak, for your business.

Similar to your EIN at the state level, the federal government identifies your company by its data universal numbering system (DUNS) number. DUNS is a proprietary system developed and regulated by Dun & Bradstreet (D&B) that assigns a unique numeric identifier to a single business entity. In short, it is the federal tax identification number used to track your company.

In order to apply for a DUNS number go the D&B website and follow the step-by-step registration process.

When registering, you will need your EIN number and company information (name, address, phone, fax, and email address). After completing your registration, you will move on to the next step in the process—SAM.

CAUTION: Dun and Bradstreet will often contact you and attempt to upsell their additional business credit services. You DO NOT need to pay for any additional services in order to register as a vendor with the federal government.

Website: https://www.dnb.com/duns-number.html

https://www.dnb.com/duns-number.html

DUNS number is going away. The government will soon start using a unique identifier. The principal will be the same.

---

3. Standard Industrial Classification (SIC) Code

This system classifies by using a four-digit code to categorize industry areas. This is an old system that is being replaced by NAICS codes. However, because some agencies still utilize its services, you may be required to know the SIC code for your industry.

Aside from registration pages, I have not personally used the SIC code to win a government contract.

I couldn't find a search feature on the website for the SIC code. Currently, the only option for finding your code is to drill down based on more general industry titles.

Website: https://www.osha.gov/pls/imis/sicsearch.html

4. Federal Supply & Product Service Codes FSC/PSC Codes

Product service codes, also referred to as federal supply codes, are used by the government to describe the products, services, research, and development purchased by the government. Essentially, when the government pays for one of the above services or products, these codes are essentially how they track the information for the services and/or products being used.

This is different from the NAICS codes as it is only four digits, categorizes research and development (R&D), and has only specific products and services available under PSC/FSC codes. From the website, you must click a category to see its expanded subset of four digit product supply codes.

Website: https://www.acquisition.gov/sites/default/files/ page_file_uploads/PSC%20Manual%20-%20Final%20-%20 11%20August%202011.pdf

5. System for Award Management (SAM)

The acronym SAM, commonly used to describe the System for Award Management, was rolled out in 2012 to consolidate multiple vendor registrations: CCR/FedReg, ORCA, and EPLS.

SAM is now the official registration portal for anyone wanting to become a government contractor for the United States. The government has a SAM user guide that can be downloaded. Here is what you'll need to do:

1. Go to www.sam.gov

2. Create an individual account and login.

3. Click "Register New Entity" under "Register/ Update Entity" on your "My SAM" page.

4. Select your type of entity.

5. Select "Yes" to "Do you wish to bid on contracts?"

6. Complete "Core Data."

7. Complete "Assertions."

8. Complete "Representations and Certifications."

9. Complete "Points of Contact."

Your entity will become active three to five days later, when the IRS validates your EIN/TIN information.

Website: https://www.sam.gov/SAM/

NOTE: There are many tutorials on the SAM webpage regarding the registration process. There is also a phone number you can call that will guide you through the formal process and answer any questions you may have.

SMALL BUSINESS PROGRAM SITES

Throughout history, we've seen evidence supporting the theme that small businesses are the backbone of the American economy. Some statisticians state that as much as 50 percent of all new jobs are created by small businesses—for that reason, the federal government, with the help of the Small Business Administration (SBA), has set forth small business goals for every purchase that a federal agency makes.

The goal here is to ensure that small businesses get their fair share of work with each agency. For details and program requirements of each category, you can visit the specific websites below or head over to the SBA page.

Below, you'll find a breakdown of the four main categories of small business goals. Every federal agency and prime contractor must meet or exceed these goals when procuring services.

	Goals	FY 2018	FY 2019
US Contract Spending	-	$520,000,000,000	$593,000,000,000
Prime contracts for small businesses	23%	$119,600,000,000	$136,360,000,000
*Small disadvantages businesses	5%	$26,000,000,000	$29,650,000,000
*Women owned small businesses	5%	$26,000,000,000	$29,650,000,000
*HUBZone small businesses	3%	$15,600,000,000	$17,790,000,000
*Service-disabled veteran owned small businesses	3%	$15,600,000,000	$17,790,000,000

*Includes both prime contracts and subcontracts.

With numbers so ginormous, you can easily see how simple it would be to end up with a $1M - $5M contract and no one to even notice.

Contract spending continues to rise, in 2018 federal spending was only $438 billion.

6. 8(a) Business Development Program

This program is for small and disadvantaged business owners. To be eligible, small business owners must meet certain personal net worth and income requirements.

The 8(a) Business Development Program is a nine-year strategy intended to grow a small company into a medium to large business. The intent is to build up firms so that they can actively compete in open-market solicitations upon graduation. This program offers many set-aside contracts and can award sole source contracts up to $5 million. It has been dubbed in many circles a "license to steal."

Out of all the major programs, this is by far the one that is most widely used and understood in the government arena.

This program is so successful for some businesses that they actually complete and excel in the program prior to the nine-year expiration date. In essence, they have exceeded their size standard (small business revenue threshold) for being deemed a small and disadvantaged business. For a construction company, that would mean averaging more than $100,000,000 in annual revenues over a three-year period. When this happens, the SBA removes the firm from the program and they can no longer receive sole-source or set-aside contracts.

Website: https://www.sba.gov/federal-contracting/contracting-assistance-programs/8a-business-development-program

7. Women-Owned Small Business 8(m) (WOSB) Program

The program consists of two categories, Women-Owned Small Business (WOSB) and Economically Disadvantaged Women-Owned Small Business (EDWOSB). Implemented by the SBA in 2011, the WOSB/EDWOSB gained much-needed foundation after many years of being overlooked.

The program is self-registration. However, you must verify you meet the criteria of the certification by validating your credentials through an SBA-approved third-party agency.

Unlike other set-aside programs, WOSB and EDWOSB have no mentor-protégé program and no sole-source awards.

Qualified firms must have 51 percent ownership by the women in order to be eligible. Misrepresentation by husbands labeling their wives as owners of the company, when they have a full-time career in another field, is not acceptable. Check the program rules and guidelines for additional requirements.

Website: https://www.sba.gov/federal-contracting/contracting-assistance-programs/women-owned-small-business-federal-contracting-program

8. HUBZone Program

The HUBZone program is named after federally designated and historically underutilized business areas in which the U.S. government recognizes the need to create meaningful impacts to businesses and people in those communities. These areas are mapped out via the U.S. Census reports and are located throughout the country.

In order to qualify, one must operate their primary business in a federally designated HUBZone and have no less than 35 percent of their employees live in a HUBZone. Maps delineating these HUBZones are online and can be checked by inputting in the address of your business and employee address. Much like the 8(a) program, HUBZone has sole-source contracts. The target goal is five percent of all contracts.

Website: https://www.sba.gov/federal-contracting/
contracting-assistance-programs/hubzone-program

9. Service-Disabled Veteran-Owned Small Biz (SDVOSBC)

Veteran Owned Small Business (VOSB) and Service-Disabled Veteran-Owned Small Business Concerns (SDVOSBC) are the government's means of paying honor to the men and women who served this country. The government knows that military personnel are three times less likely to find a job than a civilian. An injured or disabled person is also two times less likely to be hired than a non-disabled person.

In 2003, the government created the Veterans Business Act, which established a procurement program for SDVOSBC that awards sole-source and set-aside contracts where certain criteria are met.

Both programs give contract preference to VOSB and SDVOSBC. In fact, when dealing with certain agencies like the VA hospital system, a SDVOSBC will have first priority over any other type of preference program. The goals for SDVOSBC vary depending upon the agency. The target goal is five percent of business contracts.

Many firms have tried to misrepresent themselves as SDVOSBC in an attempt to secure contracts and have been convicted of fraud.

Website: https://www.va.gov/osdbu/

PURCHASE VEHICLE SITES (WHAT THE GOVERNMENT WANTS TO BUY)

The government procures services and commodities, in hundreds, if not thousands, of ways. I don't think it's even possible for any one person to keep track of the various vehicles they use. However, the point of this section is to hone in on the places where agencies are spending the most. The nine sites listed in this section will have listed nearly 60 percent of all the government procurement that is out there.

I know that we want to have access to 100 percent of the information, but, unfortunately, our government doesn't work that way. There is NO single location that has 100 percent of all contract opportunities listed. FPDS would be the closest site (with about 90 percent of the data) that details federal monies spent by agency and contractor, but it is reported only after the deal is done. Since we are looking at opportunities on the front end, that data does us no good.

I would like to put things into perspective again using the $450 billion annual spending on contracts. Sixty percent of that would be $270 billion. Rather than concentrating on what we are missing, how about we start with trying to win some of those contracts first?

10. Beta.Sam.Gov formerly (Federal Business Opportunities [FBO])

Beta.sam.gov is the primary search engine for the majority of all federal contracts that are publicly listed over $25,000. You can search for both opportunities and awards. Beta.sam.gov is a helpful research tool to learn how the government structures contracts, makes awards, and also finds opportunities for partnerships.

Currently there are more than 92 agencies listed on the site who post the majority of their solicitations on beta.sam. Another way that federal agencies use the site is to gather market research regarding which type of small business program to set aside their solicitation for before releasing it. You will see this in the form of Sources Sought and RFI notices.

Beta.sam is no stranger to the 80/20 rule. The majority of the solicitations are handled by 18 top agencies of the 92. The top three agencies—the Department of the Navy, Defense Logistics Agency, and Department of the Air Force—handle nearly 50 percent of all solicitations on the site.

Top 18 Agencies (not in chronological order)

- Department of Navy
- Department of Air Force
- Defense Logistics Agency
- Department of Army
- General Service Administration
- Department of Homeland Security
- Agency for International Development
- Defense Information Systems Agency
- Department of Agriculture
- Department of Commerce
- Department of Energy

- Department of Labor

- Department of Treasury

- Department of Interior

- Department of Health and Human Services

- Department of Transportation

- Department of Veteran Affairs

- Department of Justice

Even though the beta.sam is the number-one location for researching federal opportunities, research shows that more than 40 percent of all federal contracts have one or no bidders. Translation: these are projects that were never listed publicly. They were typically sole-sourced to a company or packaged into a much larger contract where it was distributed to only the qualifying members. I can attest to having won contract awards that were never listed on beta.sam.

Website: https://beta.sam.gov/

Beta.sam is a work in progress. While it does not have all the features of FBO it is improving. With the eventual combination of FPDS NG it will become the premiere database for all federal opportunities over time.

---

11. General Services Administration (GSA)

The General Services Administration (GSA) was established in 1949 by Harry Truman when he consolidated the National Archives Establishment, the Public Buildings Administration, the Federal Works Agency, the War Assets Administration, the Bureau of Federal Supply, and the Office of Contract Settlement into one federal agency–the GSA.

GSA's mission is to "deliver the best value in real estate, acquisition, and technology services to government and the American people." GSA constructs, preserves, manages government buildings, promotes government operations through the development of new policies, and streamlines government purchasing. GSA provides equipment, tools, and vehicles to the military and provides state and local governments with equipment for law enforcement, rescue, and disaster recovery operations.

Website: https://d2d.gsa.gov/report/
fas-schedule-sales-query-plus-ssq

12. GSA Reverse Auction

Launched in 2014, the GSA is a government-managed reverse auction platform designed to help agencies conduct reverse auctions through multiple award schedules and select blanket purchase agreements (BPAs) for commodities.

In order to participate, small firms must be participating in a current GSA award schedule or BPA.

Website: https://reverseauctions.gsa.gov/reverseauctions/
reverseauctions/

13. Onvia

Onvia is a subscription-based website that sends out daily government bid and RFP notifications. They claim to have a searchable database of agencies and vendor profiles, as well as active projects and past contract awards.

ERIC COFFIE

I think that they are great at being a one-stop shop for state, local, and educational bid opportunities—as that information is difficult to collect and catalog. For example, here in Miami, Florida, we have unincorporated Dade County, the City of Miami, and then 30+ additional municipalities that all have their own procurement offices. Broward County is similar with 31 municipalities. Even though there are job boards, the information is still not sorted in any manner.

In terms of federal procurement, I find it hard to believe that Onvia has more public information than Federal Business Opportunities (FBO).

Besides the local and state opportunities, I say to give Onvia a try, because of the following two reasons:

- Market research is key to developing your book of business. If the site allows you to perform agency research and data mining, it's worth its weight in gold.
- Try and identify non-FBO published federal projects. Those are the ones that are more difficult to find and certainly are not cataloged.

For either of those two reasons, Onvia would be a worthwhile investment.

Website: https://www.deltek.com/en/products/business-development/govwin

14. Unison Global (formerly FedBid)

Unison global is a multifunctional business commerce platform used by governments, educational institutions, and various businesses. The former site Fedbid was created in 1999 for private sectors and government agencies looking for innovative ways to

22

purchase the goods and services they need in the most fiscally-responsible way possible. In 2019 FedBid changed its name to Unison Global and is currently managing nearly $10 billion in contracts.

Using this website, you can enter real-time reverse auctions as well as connect and collaborate with different sellers and buyers. Here is how one can use Unison Global in the most efficient way possible:

Determine the buy specifications for the services or products you are looking to purchase. Or, if you are a seller, provide the relevant information about the services or goods you offer.

Post your buy or offer to a selected community. Don't forget to ask and answer these questions:

- Receive and compare customized bids.
- Select the seller/buyer you want to award and seal the deal. Keep a compliant record for your files.

Website: https://www.unisonglobal.com/product-suites/acquisition/marketplace/

15. DIBBS: DLA Internet Bid Board System

DIBBS is a web-based application you can use to search, view, or submit secure quotes on Requests For Quotations (RFQs) for Defense Logistics Agency items. This web-based application was created to give people an opportunity to search and view various information related to DLA, like requests for proposals or awards.

Use your username and password to login or create a new account to view more information and refer to the "Help" section that features an FAQ and online help when you have trouble navigating this website.

Website: https://www.dibbs.bsm.dla.mil/dodwarning.
aspx?goto=/

16. Navy Electronic Commerce Online (NECO)

Register online with NECO as a vendor to start receiving daily emails of procurement opportunities.

You will need your DUNS number and CAGE code to register. CAGE codes are assigned when you register in the SAM.gov system.

Non-registered NECO users can browse current business opportunities. The site is considered non-secure so just be aware that when you click the link you must go to your advanced settings and then proceed.

Website: https://www.neco.navy.mil/

17. JumpStation (Federal Procurement Links)

The website offers a comprehensive list of federal acquisitions on the internet. All links are relevant and up-to-date. Use this website to find the official websites for the department of the executive branch (Department of Agriculture, Commerce, Defense, etc.), independent agencies (NASA, U.S. Postal Service, Social Security Administration), and more.

Other important links are also included—use this website to find out where you can search and apply for federal grants or explore endless opportunities for your business with federal-wide resources.

Website: https://prod.nais.nasa.gov/pub/fedproc/home.
html

18. GSA FSSI

The Federal Strategic Sourcing Initiative (FSSI) is a part of the General Services Administration (GSA) and was implemented in 2005. FSSI aims to analyze the spending pattern of federal organizations to reduce costs, improve performance, and improve purchasing power.

The goals of the FSSI include increasing savings and socioeconomic participation, sharing best practices, and promoting industry collaboration. FSSI analyzes duplicate contracts and price variations in an effort to centralize and streamline government spending. The results of the FSSI in recent years have included improved management of government purchased goods and services, cost savings, enhanced visibility regarding purchasing, and the institution of best-practice guidelines.

Website: https://www.gsa.gov/buying-selling/
purchasing-programs/federal-strategic-sourcing-initiative-fssi

EVENT WEBSITES

A ttending a government event is the single most powerful form of prospecting future clients in the federal marketplace. It is the highest and best use of your time for growing, nurturing, and cultivating relationships in the government arena.

Throughout the calendar year there are more than 1,000 events scheduled, so choose your events carefully. I encourage you to start with events recommended by the OSDBU in your area. Find the nearest OSDBU close to your city or region and ask them for a list of events.

Whichever agency buys your products or services, ask their small business specialist for a list of events to attend.

Do not underestimate the significance of attending, participating and marketing at government events.

19. Govevents.com (Government event websites)

If I had to choose a place to search for government events, the internet is the place I'd start. It is the premier location for all things government. It appears that some agencies are primarily listing their events on the web.

With that being said, I want to caution you that some types of events may not be related specifically to contracting. Many events are being held for government agencies, representatives, and organizations that want to influence policy. For me, this is high-level work not for those who are just starting to break into a market.

If you are looking for a smorgasbord of events, then start here and browse around.

Website: http://govevents.com

20. Business USA

Business USA has changed over to USA.gov, which is a platform that provides information related to U.S. Government services. They cover areas like disabilities, disasters, grants and loans, legal, small business and taxes, military veterans, jobs, unemployment, housing, and much more.

I have never used them as a resource but you should as it seems much more consumer friendly. For example, you can check the status of your federal tax refund, register to vote, or file unemployment.

But the reason why someone may want to use the site is to search for events. At the top of the page in the search bar if you type in the word "events," they will display a list of upcoming events.

Website: https://www.usa.gov/business?source=busa

21. Federal Business Council

The Federal Business Council appears to have an event almost every day. The majority of their events have a technology theme, and each of them are held at government locations throughout the nation with thousands of federal employees in attendance. Events feature the latest in technological advances, military hardware, and training.

These tradeshows are touted as a way of developing relationships in order to better understand agency needs. The events invite participants to connect with agencies that are on their target market list and help facilitate pre-event marketing. They have account managers available to assist you in this process.

Out of the three event sites listed this is where I would spend my time and energy.

Website: https://www.fbcinc.com/search.aspx

22. Other Places to FIND Events

Alternative websites to seek strategic conferences and matchmaking events include:

- DOD OSDBU (https://business.defense.gov/Small-Business/)
- Beta.sam.gov (https://beta.sam.gov/) (MOVED)
- Washington Technology (https://washingtontechnology.com/Home.aspx)
- Eventbrite https://www.eventbrite.com/
- PTAC events https://www.aptac-us.org/

Networking and relationships are key to growing your contract business! Being at the location of the industry leaders and decision makers in your space will be vital to your success. In fact, capture management and business development are all about networking with key decision makers. This is the lifeblood of a successful federal contractor.

DATA/MARKET RESEARCH (TOOLS) SITES

Who buys your products? How much do they spend per year? This chapter explores the ways in which you can locate information on previous contracts, understand what your competitors are doing, and what the government has planned for the future.

Government contracting, much like any business, is all about relationships. I have learned that one of the best ways to identify potential relationships is through market research.

Once you have identified your product or service and the agency/contractor that is buying your services, it's imperative that you contact and market to those persons. This is the basis for this chapter—where to find and identify potential partners, suppliers, and customers for relationship development.

23. SBA Dynamic Small Business Search

This is one of my most frequently used websites for market research on small businesses. It is the federal database for SBA registered small businesses.

All organizations that are currently registered in the 8(a) Business Development and HUBZone programs are listed in this database. The site also maintains former SBA registered small businesses.

Personally, I've used this site to identify:

• Local, small business partners for contract opportunities in other state.

- Partners who have certifications that I may not have opportunities for (in my local area).
- Firms who have been successful with small business programs (to recruit potential staff members).
- Companies who are finishing their 8a BD program term with potential contracts.

If you want to jumpstart growth in the federal marketplace, this is one of the premiere research tools for finding your next partner.

Website: https://web.sba.gov/pro-net/search/dsp_dsbs.cfm

NOTE: Registering in SAM does not put you into the database. Your organization must be approved via the SBA DLS system.

24. Federal Procurement Data System (FPDS)

This is another big player in my market research toolbox. The Federal Procurement Data System (FPDS) is the database of ALL federal procurement spending. Every time a federal agency initiates a "buy" action to procure goods or services, they are required to record that action into a system that ultimately ends up here (in the FPDS system). The FPDS then records that information into a database that it catalogs it into 12 categories:

- Contracting office code
- Program/funding office code
- NAICS code
- PSC code
- DUNS number
- Contractor information
- Country code

- Country name
- Principal place of performance
- Location, state, and code
- Principal place of performance name, ZIP code, and program
- System equipment codes

When using the site, all of the information can be sorted and searched by any of these 12 categories. It can also be parsed, sorted, and manipulated in any way that you like. With a quick search of your NAICS codes, you can easily find a list of the top 10 agencies that buy your products and the top 10 vendors that sell your product to the government.

Website: https://www.fpds.gov/fpdsng_cms/index.php/en/

25. Past Performance Information Retrieval System

The Past Performance Information Retrieval System (PPIRS)—or "P-e-e-P-u-r-s," as we say phonetically in the world of federal contracting—was designated as the repository of past performance data. Here you receive a report card for how well you perform on a job.

PPIRS was created to comply with FAR regulation 42.1503(4) (d), which essentially states that the requirement to catalog contractor performance data is required only under certain conditions. For example, for construction, it is recommended that PPIRS be used for all contracts of $700,000 or more, or a contract that was terminated by default.

I've learned from personal experience that when you are doing well as a contractor, you want to encourage your contract

31

officer representative to input your history into your PPIRS website. It will immensely help when being considered for Indefinite Delivery Indefinite Quantity Contracts (IDIQs).

I know of contractors who have failed to perform and PPIRS did not prevent them from receiving other source selection opportunities. Instead, it is available as a tool if a contracting agency or office is leveraging one firm over another. But, for the most part, if they know your firm and have experience working with your organization, a negative PPIRS review will not prevent you from receiving other contracts.

Website: https://www.cpars.gov/

26. Federal Buyers Guide

As a leader in global business communications, Federal Buyers Guide Inc. is well-known in the B2G directory publishing space. It was founded in 1979 and has transitioned into a government marketing services company that targets online, digital, and print media. Their main goal as a trusted third party is to connect various businesses with the government and to help these groups communicate and collaborate with one another. All content of Federal Buyers Guide is sorted by region and industry, which makes it easy to search and access the information you are most interested in.

Website: https://www.hugedomains.com/domain_profile. cfm?d=govsupplier&e=com

27. GSA Schedule Sales Query

The GSA Schedules E-Library provides contract award information for the General Services Administration. This is the database of the federal supply contractors for GSA schedule holders. When using the online library, a search can be conducted by using a keyword, the contractor's name, the contract number, the schedule/SIN/GWAC number, or the NAICS.

A search will return a source number, category, and description for all potential matches. Additional details regarding a possible match can be viewed by clicking on the category or source number. In addition to the general search, the GSA Schedules E-Library also offers a contractor directory organized alphabetically. A cross-schedule search tool is available to locate providers that provide contract coverage under multiple schedules.

Contractors report the information that is queried; thus, it is only as good as the people inputting the information. If the contractor fails to input the information, then there is simply nothing to search.

Website: https://d2d.gsa.gov/report/
fas-schedule-sales-query-plus-ssq

28. Vetbiz

Here you'll find information on registering to become a Veteran-Owned Small Business (VOSB) and a Service-Disabled Veteran-Owned Small Business Concern (SDVOSBC).

Before you become registered as a vendor, your first must go through verification. Verification is the process that Service-Disabled Veteran-Owned Small Businesses and Veteran-Owned Small Businesses must undergo in order to qualify for VA set-aside contracts. This process is managed by the Center for Verification and Evaluation (CVE) but is transitioning to the MyVA system.

On the front page of the website, you'll see a list of conferences and events. There, you are also able to explore the means of registering as a VOSB or SDVOSBC and how to get verified. The site also links to forecast opportunities and Veteran Business Centers to help vets gain more access to contract opportunities.

Website: https://www.va.gov/osdbu/

29. USA Spending

Do not confuse USAspending.gov with USAspending.com. They are totally different sites, as you will find out if you accidentally clicked on the latter. USAspending.gov is the government-sponsored and endorsed platform that offers transparency on how the government is spending our taxpayer dollars. It is also the place where I performed research that was quoted in early sections of the book.

This site offers users research data that is more macro-level spending. Here you can also view data related to grants, loans, and other financial assistance category spending.

A quick glimpse will show you that in FY2015 the government spent $438B in contracts, $616B in grants, $4.6B in loans, and $1.7 trillion in other financial assistance.

For persons looking to find micro-level information on how the specifics contract breakdown and details of the spending, I would refer you back to the FPDS site.

Website: https://www.usaspending.gov/#/

30. ASSIST

ASSIST contains more than 114,000 indexed technical specifications, standards, military handbooks, and other technical documents used by the Department of Defense.

> **PRACTICAL USE: If you are designing a project for a federal agency this is where you would go to access reference material for your design. Primarily used by Architects and Engineers.**

Quick Search allows a user to conduct a search for Defense Standardization Program documents that have been cleared for public release. Data is updated every business day.

To search, you will need to enter at least one of the following: Document ID, Document Number, or Find Term (in which you are searching by a particular word or phrase).

You will then specify a date range for your search. Filter search results by selecting a status (active, inactive, active/inactive, inactive/cancelled, or cancelled) and/or a Federal Supply Class code.

If a file is available based on your search terms, a PDF icon will be visible. Click on the icon to open the document, and then save to your computer or print. A padlock icon will be visible if the document is not available for public release.

The website will show up as a non-secure site. You will need to go to your advanced settings in order to access it. As we have stated before, the government sites are not all listed in a Google search.

Website: https://assist.dla.mil/online/start/

31. Senate and House Committees

House.gov is the U.S. House of Representatives' website that lists all of the members of the House, various committees, and, most importantly, legislative action being taken.

FULL DISCLOSURE: I have never used this website to help me gather information in an effort to identify, obtain, or secure a federal contract.

At some point in your government contracting career, if your organization was impacted by one of these issues, you could attend a hearing and offer your opinion on the matter in an effort to persuade House members to change their minds for voting purposes. For the most part, though, these decisions are for influencers who stand to lose millions and billions by policy changes. This is where you would find uber lobbying for changes in the transportation policies.

Website: https://www.senate.gov/

32. Contractor Misconduct Site

This website is sponsored by an organization known as POGO, Project on Government Oversight. They have specific criteria by which they tackle issues of fraud, waste, and abuse in government.

The site lists contractors who routinely are awarded contracts from our government despite a continuous history of misconduct.

If you are working for a contractor who is not complying with the rules of FAR, then you may want to consider reporting that organization. You may also want to research the organization on this database, as they could have a history of committing similar acts to other companies.

If a government agency is the one causing you undue harm, visit the SBA website and find a local ombudsman in your area. Ombudsmen are the board on regulatory fairness and will give businesses the opportunity to have their case heard before a committee of non-related agencies, companies, and officials.

Website: https://www.contractormisconduct.org/

33. Government Accountability Office (GAO)

The government accountability office is an independent, non-partisan agency that works for Congress. As per their website, GAO is often called the "Congressional watchdog," examining how taxpayer dollars are spent and providing Congress and federal agencies with information to help the government save money and work efficiently.

Most often, the GAO issues detailed reports outlining specific problems within federal agencies. Items range from improper spending to limited accountability and improper reporting and a host of other issues. These reports are often scathing and elicit a conversation at the Congressional level and within the agency to make changes, improvements, and recommendations.

When looking at how to solve massive problems within government this is a great place to turn for clearly identified and articulated problems at federal agencies. By understanding the size and complexity of a problem, contractors can propose solutions that rectify the findings by GAO improving the agency's standing with Congress.

Website: https://www.gao.gov/

34. GSA Public Spend Category Management Dashboards

One way that the government is buying hundreds of billions annually is through the use of Best-in-Class (BIC) acquisition solutions. By definition, BIC acquisition designations identifies government-wide contracts that satisfy key criteria defined by the Office of Management and Budget (OMB). Essentially, these are large pooled contracts where multiple vendors pre-qualify to be eligible to compete over a fixed period of time, typically 10 years.

Currently, there are 10 categories that include 39 BIC solutions. The 10 categories include: professional services, IT, travel, transportation & logistics, medical, industrial products & services, human capital, facilities & construction, security & protection, and office management.

A recently launched tool, use this portal to be able to search who is winning these contracts or task orders in an effort to do your market research for both current and future opportunities.

Website: https://d2d.gsa.gov/report/ public-category-management-dashboards-analytics

35. Epipeline

Most of the services that have already been described at this point were all free services sponsored or created by government agencies. However, Epipeline is a subscription-based service that performs market research for your firm based on a specific set of criteria.

From my own browsing of the website, it appears that they have been data-mining federal business operations throughout history in order to extract future predictions for market demand. They claim to aid in identifying, qualifying, and managing government opportunities prior to being released in the public domain.

The site is owned by Government Contracts USA who is also affiliated with Governmentbids.com, Bidnet, and IPT. For that reason, I would conclude that they are a credible organization in the federal marketplace and not a fly-by-night company.

Website: https://www.epipeline.com/

36. Proxity

The National Stock Number Contract (NSN) is officially recognized by the United States government, the North Atlantic Treaty Organization (NATO), and many governments around the world. Federal agencies, including the Department of Defense (DOD), use the NSN to buy and manage billions of dollars worth of supplies yearly. Currently there are more than 6 million NSNs in the federal supply system.

With that vast count of NSN it can be difficult for someone to figure out exactly the part or component that the agency is requesting without a database of sorts. Proxity is the first website that I found who actually had a listing of ALL NSN numbers in one place. There website claims that they do other things like, Agency profiles, Teaming, millions of emails for prime and subcontractors, mil specs and standards and 3000 state and local agency solicitations.

But what I have used them for in the past was to help vendors who sell physical items match up the corresponding NSN number to the physical product. This is particularly useful when selling on the DLA board system DIBBS and occasionally on Unison Global. There is a free search feature that allows you to search expiring contracts, daily solicitations, mil specs, and five-year sales roadmap. When I input my CAGE Code it provided me with a list of similar NAICS codes, last-year awards totals by agency, number of vendors, dollars spent, and expiring contracts through for the next five years.

Website: https://www.proxity-ec.com/

37. GOVGISTICS

Another NSN search website that powers contract bidding, market research, and data export, particularly for product purchases, specifically those using NSN numbers, is GOVGISTICS. The company's website boasts having a National Stock Number and CAGE Code database procurement history spanning 70+ years. Additionally, they claim to have 33+ million NSN Data Rows, a procurement history of more than 51 million rows, and add 2,500 solicitations daily.

For free, you can perform a quick "public search" by NSN or Cage code, but it will only list out the company's name, nothing more.

Website: https://www.govgistics.com/govgistics_home.aspx

FORECAST WEBSITES
(UPCOMING OPPORTUNITIES)

Working in government contracting is much like starting a train from a standstill position. It is a long arduous process to start, but once you get started, unless you push the breaks or run off course there's no stopping it.

A contracting agent procures goods and services on behalf of his/her agency. They negotiate supplier contracts, conduct market research, resolve arising conflicts, and maintain purchase records. In the federal arena the Contracting Officer Technical Representative (COTR) serves as the contract agent. They work with contract specialists, officers and financial representatives (from the contracting office) to serve three primary functions for the government:

- Acquisition planning
- Contract formation
- Contract administration

The first step in the acquisition-planning phase is to determine the need. Furthermore, the first step under the related functions of determining the need is to allocate any forecasting requirements.

Each procurement office should have a list of upcoming needs for the next one to five years. This is known as the "forecast list." A forecast list is a report that an agency issues for planning purposes that identifies their future needs. The list will contain valuable information related to the anticipated need, such as: who will be managing the process, how much they expect it will cost, where it is located, the buyer, and so on.

Oftentimes, agencies release RFP's and solicitations with small turnaround windows for the contractor to respond. By having access to the forecast list, you can adequately prepare for any upcoming solicitations before they are officially funded and released.

Most federal agencies have an office of small and disadvantaged business utilization (OSDBU). The purpose of this office is to advocate, educate, identify, and help connect small businesses to federal agents and agencies. They host outreach events and encourage large firms to utilize small businesses in their contracts. This will also be the first place where you call, email, or visit to request a forecast list.

38. Office of Small and Disadvantaged Business Utilization

The informal OSDBU Interagency Council website has a listing of all the OSDBU members who are part of this collaborative effort.

When contacting, ask that person to connect you with the local OSDBU team member in your area. The number of OSDBU is dependent upon the amount of procurement that each agency performs. There will not always be an OSDBU in your state. You may have to travel to actually meet someone in person.

When you call the primary OSDBU phone number on the agency profile page, you will be connected to the nearest local OSDBU office site for that agency in your state, region, and ZIP code.

QUICK TIP: If the OSDBU office is on a government installation and you can't access to that installation. Follow these 3 easy steps to meet the person.

Step 1) Go to beta.sam.gov; find a solicitation with an onsite bid walkthrough for a project at that facility. Sign up to attend the pre-bid meeting.

Step 2) Schedule a meeting with the OSDBU for the same date as the pre-bid meeting.

Step 3) After the pre-bid conference, drive over to the OSDBU office.

Website: https://www.usa.gov/business?source=busa

Note: *This tip was written BC (before COVID), prior to everything going virtual. However, when things get back to normal and you need to do one-on-one meetings this tip will come in handy.*

39. Acquisition Central Forecasts of Federal Opportunities

This is a diverse website that has tons of information. Here you will find a centralized location that directly links agency forecast lists, OSDBU, and specific business opportunities.

Some of the agencies on the OSDBU's list may or may not be a part of the OSDBU Council. Use this list to supplement the one that you have in building your Target Market List (TML).

Website: https://www.acquisition.gov/procurement-forecasts

40. CDC OSDBU Contact List

The Department of Health and Human Services rounds out the top 10 list of agencies on Federal Business Opportunities. The agency purchases a plethora of products and utilizes a host of recurring services.

Like most agencies that are non-DOD, they outsource mostly all major construction to the U.S. Army Corps of Engineers. But any minor renovations are probably good, "low-hanging fruit" that you can procure under simplified acquisition or credit card purchase.

Website: https://www.hhs.gov/

41. DOD OSDBU POC

This is the Department of Defense (DOD) website for their Office of Small Business Programs. As most people would guess, the bulk of the procurement actions in contracting are DOD related.

Under the Small Business Initiatives tab is a list of regional councils for small businesses. Here you will find the equivalent to an OSDBU.

The site boasts a calendar of events for classes, workshops, and conferences. Look around the website as it is an excellent resource for someone getting started. Note that under the resources tab, they have links that explain getting started in federal contracting.

Website: https://www.acq.osd.mil/osbp/

42. Business USA

Business USA is a great portal website with thousands of pages to explore in the world of doing business. The site itself boasts a section for government contracting.

They teach classes on starting a business, exporting, disaster assistance, and a gamut of other things.

On the site, you can view a map of PTAC's offices and Business Assistance Centers near your location. They also have a list that links OSDBU offices and forecast information to more than two dozen agencies.

Website: https://www.usa.gov/business?source=busa

43. FedMarket

FedMarket offers numerous sales resources for government contractors. On their official website, they offer GSA schedule proposal solutions to meet your unique needs, consulting, and training along with online help. You can view a full training calendar here and find the training or seminar near you.

Use this website to learn more about the proposals, including services, writing software, relevant templates and examples—or browse the free content such as complimentary webinars and whitepapers. You can stay in touch with FedMarket by subscribing to their newsletter or following their blog, which is updated regularly.

I must forewarn you that they will try and sell you various services that can be helpful but not necessary.

Website: https://www.fedmarket.com/

44. Federal Interagency Databases Online (Forecasts)

This location offers an advanced acquisition search for the Department of Commerce. It allows a person to search by a specific agency under the Department of Commerce, dollar range, NAICS code, contract method, or acquisition vehicle.

In my personal opinion, the website is bland and there is no additional content of significant value other than the search feature.

Website: http://govwebs.net/fido/

45. America's Combat Logistics Support Agency

Defense Logistics Agency (DLA) has the third most contract opportunities listed in FBO (only behind the Navy and Air Force). The DLA website is probably one of the best federal websites for providing information and resources to small businesses. It is a great place to get started in your federal journey.

In the small business subsection (https://www.dla.mil/SmallBusiness/) of the website, you can download a book on how to get started working with the DLA. If you scroll to the bottom of the page you'll find a complete listing of all DLA Small Business Offices around the country.

The DLA website is one of the few agencies that have their own bid board system which we discussed earlier in the book.

Website: https://www.dla.mil/SmallBusiness/

46. Naval Facilities Engineering Command / NAVFAC's

The Naval Facilities Engineering Command's (NAVFAC) primary business lines include asset management, capital improvements, contingency engineering, environmental, expeditionary, and public works.

NAVFAC worldwide is broken into three areas:

- **NAVFAC Pacific** which includes Far East, Marianas, and Hawaii.

- **NAVFAC Atlantic** which includes Europe Africa, Southeast Asia, Mid-Atlantic, Southeast, Southwest, and Washington.

- **NAVFAC Specialty Centers** which include the Engineering and Expeditionary Warfare Center and the Crane Center.

The vast amount of procurement opportunities is just as wide ranging in scope as they are in location.

Website: https://www.navfac.navy.mil/products_and_services/sb/opportunities.html

47. Treasury Small Business Office

The Department of Treasury is in the top 20 percent of agencies by the number of solicitations listed on FBO.

Remember the 80/20 rule. The top 20% of agencies account for 80% of all contract spending.

The small business office site (OSDBU) does have a webcast on how to do business with the Treasury Department. With a quick glance of the website you'll find long-term contracts that are ending within the next two years. You will also find a list of their small business goals, and an outline of outreach activities amongst other helpful resources that small businesses need to break into the market and win them as clients.

For small businesses out there doing community projects or manufacturing, the Department of Treasury has a few programs (State Small Business Credit Initiative, Small Business Lending Funding, and Community Development Financial Institutions Funding) that support public and private partnership and offer private sector loans.

Website: https://home.treasury.gov/policy-issues/ small-business-programs

48. Forecast list for GSA projects

This used to be a simple website that provided forecasts of contracting opportunities for GSA projects not prior to be listed on FBO. Through the newly named, **Acquisition Gateway,** you can search the national database for upcoming contract opportunities before the solicitations are posted on-line. You are able to search by agency, award status, location, and NAICS codes.

A forecast map of upcoming contract opportunities is available from the website. This is how you get ahead of a project and put together a team to pursue the opportunity prior to its release.

The GSA is the largest manager and overseer of government buildings in the world! They also maintain the largest buyers' hand guide of products and services via the GSA schedule. So they are no small fish when it comes to government contracting. GSA is a monster on their own merit when it comes to federal procurement.

Website: https://www.gsa.gov/buying-selling/
forecast-of-contracting-opportunities

FREE RESOURCES

Mostly everything in the government is FREE. All of the program registrations are FREE, as are all the certifications, online databases, freedom of information act requests, etc. The challenge is the platforms and systems are bulky, outdated, cumbersome, not user friendly, and require expertise for people to navigate through these murky waters. With that said, there are government-sponsored organizations designed to help provide technical assistance for people and companies wanting to venture out into the world of federal contracting.

49. Procurement Technical Assistance Centers (PTAC)

The Procurement Technical Assistance Centers (PTAC) is a national agency that provides counselors to help with teaching and guiding companies in the world of doing business with the government. There are more than 300 PTAC offices around the country. They are in nearly every state and most major cities. So, most likely, you won't have to travel very far to find one close to your city.

As with most agencies, some PTAC counselors have more experience and are better than others. PTAC can help with obtaining small business certifications, navigating SAM, GSA, contract accounting, proposal writing, teaming, and subcontracting.

Website: https://www.aptac-us.org/

50. Small Business Development Centers (SBDC)

Regarding themselves as the "most comprehensive small business assistance network in the United States and its territories," the goal of America's Small Business Development Centers (SBDCs) is to assist entrepreneurs on the realization of their business objectives. The network includes over 1,000 service centers that provide low-cost training and free consulting. Training topics include: writing business plans, marketing, technology development, international trade, accessing capital, and regulatory compliance.

To locate a local SBDC, interested parties can visit the website, click on the home tab, and then click on *find your SBDC*. Visitors will then be provided with the option to search by ZIP code.

Website: http://floridasbdc.org/

51. Women's Owned Business Centers (WOBC)

Women's Owned Business Centers was created for women across the nation who want to start their own business but don't know where to begin. It is also valuable for women small business owners who may face problems regarding training, support, assistance, and relevant information that can help overcome those issues.

Get involved and become a member of Women's Owned Business Centers with these four easy steps:

1. Fill out the membership form online or download a printable version.

2. Pay your membership fee through PayPal, or by mailing a check.

3. Get your benefits.

4. Get involved by joining a committee.

Website: https://www.wbdc.org/

52. Service Corps of Retired Executives (SCORE)

The Service Corps of Retired Executives (SCORE) is another free resource with physical locations throughout the country. SCORE is made up of a group of retired executives who lend their business experience and wisdom to small businesses. They provide training classes and workshops as well as review business and marketing plans.

Website: https://www.score.org/

LEARNING

As a guideline for providing information that will help jump-start your federal government career, we did not want to add a bunch of fluff in the book. Therefore, you will find that we chose to exclude topics such as:

- FAR – Federal Acquisition Regulations
- DFAR – Defense Federal Acquisition Regulation
- FAA procurement rules
- CFR – Code of Federal Regulations
- Federal Procurement Regulations site

As a pocket guide, we are not here to teach you every aspect of federal contracting. Nor can we provide you with all the tools needed to understand the government market in one swoop. Items such as regulations and policies can be found using a Google search and accessed fairly easy. Through this hand guide, we ensure that you are gaining only the most essential information.

53. Small Business Administration (SBA)

The first place that everyone should turn to when considering working with government contracting is the SBA.

In fact, the SBA is the government arm for doing small business in the United States. Therefore, it only make sense to default to their website.

On the site, they have excellent descriptions of the various programs and how they work. You will be able to download applications and learn about the eligibility criteria and requirements for becoming certified. But, in terms of help with the certifications or initially launching your business, their resources are limited to the contents of the site.

The SBA offices today primarily serve the participants of the various small business programs, particularly 8(a). So it would behoove you to become certified in one of the programs; that way, they can assign a dedicated 8(a) Business Development specialist to assist you in growing your business.

The Small Business Association Learning Center offers a range of internet-based training courses for small business owners free of charge. Courses require Adobe Reader and Adobe Flash Player to view. Simply visit the learning center section of the Small Business Association website to view their current offerings.

Current course topics include:

√ Taking Your High-Tech Product to Market

√ Sales: A Guide for the Small Business Owner

√ Business Opportunities: A Guide to Winning Federal Contracts

√ Contracting Opportunities for Veteran Entrepreneurs

√ Crime Prevention: A Guide for Small Businesses

√ Encore Entrepreneurs: An Introduction to Starting Your Own Business

√ How to Prepare Government Contract Proposals

√ Marketing 101: A Guide to Winning Customers

Website: https://www.sba.gov/

52. USA.gov

This website contains a list of every single federal agency and its parent agency alphabetized and indexed.

The information here is expansive; as you click through the name of the agency, it takes you to affiliate organizations and even websites of the affiliates.

Under each state, it lists the various state agencies (consumer protection office, corrections department, election office, surplus property sales, etc.) with links to the respective sites.

Website: https://www.usa.gov/

55. Govcon Giants

Probably since the beginning of capitalism there has always been someone teaching how to win at the game of capitalism. Much like any industry where there is potential for big profits, people, and companies see big opportunity in helping those who so desire. The government marketplace was no different.

When I came onto the federal contracting scene back in 2007, we struggled to find mentors, teachers, and people who wanted to help us succeed. It was a long arduous process not clearly spelled out in any one place. Even the SBA with all their funding and programs only communicated the ideas from a conceptual theoretical standpoint, not a practical one.

Fast forward to 2017 and I am scratching my own itch, building the platform that I wanted to be a part of, providing the information that I wish I had access to when I was starting out. Govcon Giants delivers the most accurate experience, sharing the journey and struggle of tackling the "govcon" world. Many students have said that we are teaching elements from the bottom up.

Most people who come from government understand program management or technology infrastructure but how to start, grow, and maintain a business requires more knowledge and experiences. Govcon Giants brings you that in the form of a blog, podcast, email marketing list, and community.

Website: http://govcongiants.com/

56. Small Govcon

Legal news and notes for small government contractors. Smallgovcon is a blog written by attorneys who work for Koprince Law. They share stories and insights into legal decisions and actions that impact the world of federal contracting.

For example, just browsing the website today you'll find discussions on how unequivocal control is required for joint ventures, removing a price realism evaluation is a material change, and a GAO ruling that the RFQ requirement unreasonably restricted competition. The information is extremely well written but may be high-level stuff for novice contractors just getting started.

On their blog, topics include 8(a), claims and appeals, GAO bid protests, SBA size protests, statues and regulations, and suspension debarment and penalties, to name a few. They have published several handbooks on several of the topics mentioned above.

If you have legal questions regarding a topic or issue, chances are you can find a similar issue posted at smallgovcon.com. The firm is also very active posting on LinkedIn with many persons citing or re-sharing their posts as references.

Website: https://smallgovcon.com/

57. The American Small Business Coalition (ASBC)

Information, relationships, and access: I am familiar with this organization because the CEO and Chief Visionary Officer Guy Timberlake is a very vocal leader in the federal community because he blogs about opportunities in government contracting.

The American Small Business Coalition hosts intelligence boot camps, business mixers, networking, and educational events around the country. As a member, you will have access to their proprietary GovCon help desk and the *A-Team* that will answer any question you have about programs, marketing, and FAR compliance.

I personally enjoy all of Guy's content as he helps walk you through finding the "low-hanging fruit" in the world of govcon. I strongly encourage everyone to join this organization.

Website: https://www.theasbc.org/

MEMBERSHIP ASSOCIATIONS/ ORGANIZATIONS

Until now, our focus has been primarily on websites that are owned and operated by federal agencies. This holds true as well in this section. There are hundreds, if not thousands, of state, regional, and local organizations around the country, but we are concentrating only on the national associations with an emphasis on the federal marketplace.

58. Minority Business Development Agency (MBDA)

The Department of Commerce governs the Minority Business Development Agency (MBDA), which is a job-creating agency that promotes the growth of a strong minority-owned business sector (now being considered an essential element of successful international trade).

The agency was originally founded as the Office of Minority Business Enterprise by the Nixon administration in 1969, but began operating under its current title in 1979. Through the numerous business centers located across the United States, the MBDA provides the following services: global business development, access to capital and financial management, access to contracts, access to markets, technical assistance, and strategic business consulting.

They host a national small business conference that hundreds of federal agencies attend to share how they do business with their organization.

This is probably the best-funded organization on our list, with a primary focus on the federal marketplace.

Website: https://www.mbda.gov/

59. National Contract Management Association (NCMA)

The National Contract Management Association (NCMA) was created for professionals in the field of contract management to advance their careers. The organization has over 20,000 members who are dedicated to professional growth and educational advancement. The main goal of NCMA is to serve and inform its members as well as offer opportunities for self-improvement and the open exchange of ideas.

Visit their website to see the professional events near you, to stay informed, or to join NCMA community. Choose your membership plan (please note that all new members pay an initial fee) and then simply click on the membership option that suits you best.

This is an organization that will help your staff fully develop an understanding of the ins and outs of your contract.

Website: https://www.ncmahq.org/

60. National Minority Supplier Diversity Council (NMSDC)

MBDA has a network of 23 regional councils and hosts dozens of events annually around the country. I would say they are the second most active organization with a federal focus (just behind MBDA). The difference is that NMSDC works with private firms in addition to government agencies.

What sets the National Minority Supplier Development Council (NMSDC) apart from other organizations is the Minority Business Enterprise (MBE) certification. Members of NMSDC have the opportunity to apply and receive an MBE certification that then gives them access to the supplier network. NMSDC has a supplier network of large firms that have committed to hiring, training, and mentoring qualified MBE firms certified through NMSDC.

With the vast network of corporations in their supplier network, they connect persons through business matchmaking events. For any small business looking to capitalize on their expertise and grow business, NMSDC is there to assist.

The NMSDC annual conference touts that they will have more than 6,000 CEOs, procurement executives, and supplier diversity professionals convening all in one place.

Website: https://nmsdc.org/

61. Society of American Military Engineers (SAME)

Society of American Military Engineers was originally founded in 1920 after the end of World War I and currently serves as the leading association for military engineers in the nation. Established by engineers, the organization has grown to include over 30,000 interdisciplinary members that are committed to maintaining and protecting national security.

Members include architects, engineers, construction workers, environmental workers, facility managers, contractors, acquisition field workers, and those in related disciplines. The mission of SAME is to "lead collaborative efforts to identify and resolve national security infrastructure-related challenges." The website features general information about SAME, a membership directory, information on joining SAME, and a calendar of regional and national events.

In many states, SAME is where you interact and have the opportunity to actually meet agency representatives, engineers, and prime contractors. They host monthly luncheons where COTRs and small business firms interact in an informal setting.

Website: https://www.same.org/

62. US Women's Chamber of Commerce (USWCC)

Margot Dorfman is a special woman who has spent the better part of her life fighting for women's right to gain access to government contracts and grow as leaders. She founded the U.S. Women's Chamber of Commerce (USWCC) after realizing the disparities in contracting for women. On their website it states that USWCC gives collective strength of women in the U.S. economy.

What I learned by interviewing her on my podcast was that USWCC remains staunchly "non captive." That means that they are driven by the interests, aspirations, and needs of the members – and not influenced by big corporations who would moderate their voice or blunt their independent work. Nothing is more indicative of that voice when they won a lawsuit against the U.S. Small Business Administration for failure to implement a law passed in 2000 to provide a targeted set aside for women-owned businesses seeking federal contracts.

In 2007, the USWCC filed a brief in support of women's class action suit against Walmart. In 2008, Margot provided testimony for Fair Pay Act of 2009 and, in 2012, listed four ways in which contract officers can improved the use of WOSB and EDWOSB.

Website: https://uswcc.org/

63. HUBZone Contractors National Council

The HUBZone Council is a nonprofit trade association comprised of a group of companies and organizations working together to improve and support the HUBZone program and small business community. Established in 2000, the HUBZone Council has been serving small businesses for over 20 years.

The HUBZone Council advocates for policies that bring opportunities to the thousands of communities that lack capital investment on Capitol Hill and in federal agencies. As Michelle Burnett, the program's current executive director, stated on the Govcon Giants podcast, the HUBZone program is all inclusive.

It doesn't matter what color of skin you are, it doesn't matter where you're from, what you did. It's a program that allows access for anyone. It's about supporting – Michelle Burnett

I have personally attended two of their events in the past and found that they are well connected to federal contracting community but hold no punches when voicing their concern for small business matters. Their focus includes, legislative reform, economic and community development, and increasing HUBZone spending.

Website: https://hubzonecouncil.org/about

64. National 8(a) Association

The National 8(a) Association helps certified businesses by providing valuable networking tools, education, and the guidance companies need to thrive and grow. Their regular meetings and events, along with the national summer conference, are attended by hundreds of entrepreneurs and businesspeople who want to gain further education, promotion, or up-to-date federal contracting information.

Visit their website to get involved and become a member of the National 8(a) Association. Register for an upcoming conference, business fair, and any other event online (or donate for a cause). Please note that their membership is open to all organizations, 8(a) and non-8(a) firms alike, regardless of affiliation, and requires that every member to pay annual member dues.

Website: https://www.national8aassociation.org/

65. National Association of Small Business Contractors (NASBC)

The American Small Business Chamber of Commerce is the outgrowth of the National Association of Small Business Contractors. You will find both names throughout the website.

On their site, they claim to be the nation's leading trade association representing small business contractors.

Just by browsing the site, you will find business matches, agency network connections, workshops, events, meetings, and courses. Through their network navigator, they connect you to the National Veteran Business Council and Economic Development Centers in regional areas around the United States.

Woman-owned small businesses could get certified in the WOSB/EDWOSB program through an affiliate third-party partner organization, the U.S. Women's Chamber of Commerce.

Website: http://www.nasbc.org/

66. Native American Contractors Association (NACA)

NACA promotes common interests of tribally-owned corporations, Native Hawaiian Organizations (NHO), and Alaska Native Corporations (ANC). They promote the benefits of using some of the nearly 240,000 Native-owned firms in the federal marketplace.

If you qualify for one of these groups, the SBA 8(a) BD program has many advantages for Native 8(a) firms over and above the normal 8(a) BD program member participants. Visit the site, join the organization, and learn because your ceiling is limitless.

Website: https://www.nativecontractors.org/

67. Washington Technology: Contracting News

This is the place to go for news related back to the Hill. They have articles that touch on every topic that would apply to any entity doing business with the government.

The site boasts top rankings of 8(a) contractors, federal contractors, mergers, and acquisitions.

However, the site is NOT free. In order to read many of the articles, you must become a Washington Technology insider (current annual rate of $359.00). The insider benefits include discounts to media events, seminars, and summits.

Website: https://washingtontechnology.com/Home.aspx

68. GovLoop

Referred to as the knowledge network for government, GovLoop connects more than 200,000 active members—comprised of federal, state, and local government workers.

The site contains a mixture of new ideas and success stories collaborating on best practices for both individuals and agencies in their various arenas across all three levels of government. The site appears to be written by government agencies for government agencies.

The value in this marketplace is learning about questions, ideas, and other information that these officials are seeking.

The site is not restricted to only government workers, so anyone can register.

Website: https://www.govloop.com/

69. Daily Contract Posting

On the site, you can find activities related to the current Secretary of Defense—speeches, news, and press advisories. But for me, the real value is in the daily contract award winners.

At 5 p.m. each business day, all contracts valued at $7 million or more are announced in a press release. Click on the date you desire, and below is the company name, award amount, description of services provided, and the estimated completion date.

On the website, you can also subscribe to their email list and receive this information directly in your inbox.

FYI: In my book *How to Win Government Contract in 30 Days or Less*, I discuss specific tactics on how to utilize Daily Contract Posting.

Website: https://www.defense.gov/Newsroom/Contracts/

GRANTS

70. Small Business Innovation Research (SBIR) Grants

Small Business Innovation Research (SBIR) is a set-aside program for small business to engage in federal research and development with the potential for commercialization.

Small Business Technology Transfer (STTR) is a sister set-aside program to facilitate cooperation between small business concerns and national research institutions with the potential for commercialization.

There are a total of 11 participating agencies who contributed ~ $2 billion in FY 2015 to SBIR and nearly $1 billion to STTR. If you browse the site, you can view a list of award winners sorted by agency, year, and phase.

Website: https://www.sbir.gov/

71. Foundation Center (Find Grants)

This is the ultimate site to learn about philanthropy. They have foundation maps, training, an online foundation directory of more than 140,000 grant makers, and other tools and resources to help you find RFPs and learn about philanthropy.

This is the place where I recommend beginners to start and learn about grant writing.

Website: https://candid.org/?fcref=lr

72. Grants.gov

Grants.gov is a centralized location to investigate and learn about the majority of grants in the federal marketplace. It is your one-stop shop for grant research.

The site is robust and has a ton of information for anyone considering applying for a grant.

Website: https://www.grants.gov/

BUY GOVERNMENT PROPERTY

73. Government Sales and Auctions of Federal Property

Learn about surplus government sales and auctions of federal property. The site will explain where to find real estate, miscellaneous property, state auctions, federal land, and more.

You will eventually be connected to the agency website who is handling the transactions. For example, the U.S. Department of Treasury performs their own auctions for people who forget to pay their taxes or accidentally violate federal law.

Website: https://gsaauctions.gov/gsaauctions/gsaauctions/

74. Website for purchasing DOD vehicles

This is a one-stop shop for the resale of construction equipment, trucks, specialized equipment, and Humvees.

Register online, get approved, and start bidding right away. They have an email notification system that you can use to receive regular updates when new vehicles become available.

Website: https://www.gsa.gov/buying-selling/
products-services/transportation-logistics-services/
gsa-fleet-vehicle-purchasing

75. HUD Home Store

This is the U.S. Department of Housing and Urban Development (HUD) website for property sales. They have a map of your state and you can browse through the current listings of HUD properties.

All homes must be purchased through a HUD approved broker, which you can easily find on the site.

Website: https://www.hudhomestore.com/Home/Index. aspx

CONCLUSION

Whether you're just getting started or have already taken a crack at the federal marketplace, this book will save you hundreds of hours of research. No need to ask your friend how to get federal contracts. No need to subscribe to a $1,000 webinar or register to be put into some book where you will get "no-bid" contracts.

Don't fall for all the scams out there. Know the facts.

Thank you for purchasing my book. I hope that it served you well and that it continues to bring great value in your quest to win government contracts.

The money and opportunities are prime for the picking.

- $49 billion per month
- $11 billion per week
- $1.6 billion per day
- $67 million per hour
- $1.1 million every second

You have to try really hard not to get a piece of that!

APPENDIX

76. Armed Forces Communications and Electronics Association (AFCEA)

The Armed Forces Communications and Electronics Association was established in 1946 as a nonprofit membership association that focuses on cyber communications, computers, and intelligence to deal with national and international security challenges. AFCEA also offers networking opportunities, supports local chapters, sponsors events, publishes SIGNAL Magazine, promotes education, and provides various member benefits. Thanks to this program, military, government, academic, and industry communities can collaborate with each other and work on different technology and strategy issues together.

Their website provides up-to-date information about the upcoming events, member benefits, and various ways an individual can engage with AFCEA. Learn more about their community and become a member online. Their membership is available to both individuals and organizations.

Website: https://www.afcea.org/site/

77. National Association of State Procurement Officials

The National Association of State Procurement Officials, or NASPO, is an association that has procurement offices in each of the 50 states, the District of Columbia, and the territories of the United States. It was formed in 1947 by the top procurement officials. Their main goal is to improve the state procurement community through leadership, education, and communication. It's easier for the members of NASPO to achieve success as public procurement leaders because they have an instant access to the best practices, research papers, and innovative procurement strategies.

On their official website, you can take an online course, access webinars, or browse their online library full of the latest research papers and publications. Visit their main page, choose your state from the map, and learn more about that state's state procurement official, the procurement staff in their office, and how to do business with them.

Website: https://www.naspo.org/

78. National Federal Contractors Association (NAFCA)

The National Federal Contractors Association (NAFCA) is the established national trade association that focuses on small business interests and helps small federal contractors to operate and grow their businesses. By promoting and protecting the interests of small business federal contractors, NAFCA creates opportunities for business owners to improve their business in fair and reasonable competition. Their primary goal is to increase their industrial base by providing a wide range of competitive choices to government agencies.

The National Federal Contractors Association not only protects small businesses, but also fights for their interests and makes a change in the world by achieving reforms on major issues directly affecting small federal contractors. Check out their website to learn more about their cause, access their latest publications, or become a member of this constantly growing community.

Website: https://www.hugedomains.com/domain_profile.
cfm?d=nafcausa&e=com

79. Black Contractors Association

The Black Contractors Association fights for the rights of African Americans in construction, especially women and other under-represented contractors. Since African Americans do not receive a fair share of public and private contracting opportunities, this association was created to provide them with professional development opportunities, networking, information, and current trends in the industry. The members of Black Contractor Associations work together toward professional growth in the industry, equal rights, and exploring new opportunities for African Americans in construction.

Visit their website to learn more, read about available national programs, or find a chapter in your area. The National Black Contractors Association is made of eight chapters located in different states and provides its chapters and their members with professional development opportunities, current information, and trends in the industry, networking events, savings, and other services. You can also become a member online by simply printing and mailing your application. Please read their FAQ section to learn more about membership benefits.

Website: http://www.nationalbca.org/

80. Government Contractors Association

The Government Contractors Association was created to help small companies win government contracts. It's a well-known fact that small businesses, especially women owned companies and minority firms, are extremely under-represented in the government market. The Government Contractors Association offers governments contract coaching programs, news, current trends, and other information and services that help small businesses grow. Since the government is the largest consumer in the world, each company has a chance to win a government contact and improve their business.

Learn more about their events, coaching programs, and available bids online. You can also download a free book or become a member to access a sister site for the paid association members and enjoy membership benefits such as legal services, insurance programs, pharmacy discounts, etc.

Website: http://www.govcontractors.org/

81. SDVOSB Council

The primary goal of Service-Disabled Veteran-Owned Small Business Council (SDVOSBC) is to improve the business environment and increase contracting opportunities for SDVOSBs by enhancing business relationships between this community of small businesses and government contracting representatives. The Council is made up of both small and large business, SDVOSBs, and VOSBs along with federal, state, and local government agencies. They achieve their goals by providing networking opportunities, creating the environment to meet and learn, and educating their members.

Their meetings are available to anyone unless they are marked "member only." Check out their schedule online, sign up for the upcoming events, or become a member to access exclusive membership benefits and deals. The membership can expand your business by matching you with the right agencies, companies, and contractors or offering other business opportunities.

Website: http://sdvosb-council.org/

82. National Association of Minority Gov't Contractors (NAMGC)

The National Association of Minority Contractors was founded in Oakland, California in 1969, and, as of now, has the local chapters in all major cities of the United States. It's one of the oldest minority business organizations in the United States with an annual project capacity of over one billion dollars. NAMC assists its members through a network of local chapters, advocacy, education, awareness, and collaborates with strategic and corporate partners nationwide. They also organize contractor development trainings, events for their members, and workshops for the entrepreneurs who want to save money and grow their businesses.

Visit their website to learn more about their mission, sponsors, partners, and access the calendar of the upcoming events. To become a member, please find a local chapter near you and contact the chapter president.

Website: https://namcnational.org/

83. Professional Services Council

The Professional Services Council (PSC) is dubbed the voice of the government services industry. They consider themselves an advocate and resource for the federal, professional, and technical services industry.

PSC host events every week, semi-annual and annual conferences, writes policy letters, and comments and testifies on the Hill. You can be part of one of the various councils and committees, participate in leadership forums, or just follow their active Twitter site.

If I were in the professional and technical services industry as a federal contractor, this is the organization that I would want to join.

PSC is the first organization in this book of associations to maintain a magazine, *Service Contractor*. They promote and encourage active member involvement.

Websites:

https://www.pscouncil.org/

https://www.pscouncil.org/i/p/
Service_Contractor_Magazine/c/p/
ServiceContractorMagazine/Service_Contractor_.
aspx?hkey=be4f47ad-c23b-4c9c-b75b-b21f0c00108d

84. National Association of Government Contractors (NAGC)

The Government Contractors Association (GCA) is a trade association operating on the national level. The purpose of the GCA is to help contractors from small and large companies break into the government market and to provide government agencies with a means of reaching contractors when needed. Among their numerous services, GCA offers certification training, seminars, courses, mentoring opportunities, monthly meetings, and online and distance learning tools. The GCA offers federal, state, and local certification programs. Certifications include, but are not limited to, the following:

- EDWOSB certification
- SDVOSBC certification
- WOSB certification

- HUBZone certification

What I like most about NAGC is that they have publications on every aspect of government contracting. This is the only organization I found that produces their own publications explaining various aspects of government contracting.

Website: https://www.governmentcontractors.org/

RECOMMENDED RESOURCES

Guru

Guru is a freelancer marketplace in which contractors can be hired on an as-need basis to complete a wide-range of tasks. Clients can find contractors specializing in the following areas of expertise:

- Web, software, and IT
- Design, art, and multimedia
- Sales and marketing
- Writing, editing, and translation
- Engineering and architecture
- Administrative support
- Management and finance
- Legal

A client posts a job and waits for contractors to submit proposals for said job. It is free to post a job; however, for added exposure, Guru offers their "feature a job" option for $29.95.

A proposal generally includes the cost that the contractor will charge to complete the job, the time needed, and any other information that they want you to know about their services and why you should choose them over the competition. Clients have the option of privately messaging any of the contractors before making a decision if additional information is needed.

Once a contractor is hired through Guru, terms are agreed upon and the work can begin. Guru offers an escrow service referred to as "SafePay" in which the client deposits funds to be held until the work is completed. Once the work is approved, or after a set amount of time, the funds are released to the contractor. This process protects both parties. Contractors pay between 4.95-8.95 percent of their earnings to Guru, in exchange for the service. Flat rate and hourly projects are accepted.

Clients can take advantage of the workroom setting in which documents can be shared, members of a team can communicate, and milestones/tasks are defined. Freelancers can easily be rehired for future work by adding one or more milestone to a current agreement.

Website: http://www.guru.com

Upwork

Upwork is another freelancer marketplace – a much larger one than Guru. Similarly, Upwork offers an escrow service for payment protection, and the option to hire contractors on a per-project or hourly basis. Expect to weed through a large number of proposals when submitting a job posting on Upwork.

A job posting is created that outlines what is needed, the estimated budget, and any deadlines for said project. Clients can search other posted projects to get an idea of what a posting looks like. After a job is posted, clients can wait for proposals to roll in, or search through the freelancer marketplace and "invite" specific contractors to submit proposals. To help decide between contractors, clients can view the freelancer profiles and feedback scores earned from past jobs.

Job categories in Upwork are broken down as follows (with several sub categories within each main category):

- Web, mobile, and software development
- IT and networking
- Data science and analytics

- Engineering and architecture
- Design and creative
- Writing
- Translation
- Legal
- Admin support
- Customer service
- Sales and marketing
- Accounting and consulting

Upwork offers clients several membership options. The first membership level is free for clients, while freelancers pay a 10 percent project fee. Upwork Pro offers "premium talent, pre-vetted, and handpicked for you" for a fee of $149 per month and a 10 percent transaction fee paid by the client in addition to the 10 percent paid by the freelancer. The third membership level is a customizable service known as Upwork Enterprise and boasts a "customized, end-to-end Freelancer Management System." The price varies for this membership option and Upwork needs to be contacted directly for a quote. The main difference between these membership options is how much of the selection process falls on the client.

Website: https://www.upwork.com/

Virtual Staff Finder

Virtual Staff Finder is the "number-one provider of dedicated, experienced, Filipino virtual assistants" according to their website. Clients can find a virtual assistant to help with anything from small business administrative tasks to graphic design, and more.

With Virtual Staff Finder, clients follow a multi-step process to find a virtual assistant that meets their needs.

1. First, an account is created and a job description is written that describes exactly what a client is looking for.

2. Virtual Staff Finder then selects various candidates based on the posted requirements.

3. Candidates go through a testing process to ensure that they are qualified.

4. Clients interview the top three candidates.

5. Clients hire their new virtual assistant and start delegating work to them.

Virtual Staff Finder offers various business resources such as virtual assistant salary guides, outsourcing information, and lists of tasks which can be completed by a virtual assistant. All candidates undergo testing and background checks.

Virtual assistants from Virtual Staff Finder work on a monthly rate versus a per-hour rate. Once hired, payments for virtual assistants are generally made directly via PayPal.

Website: http://www.virtualstafffinder.com/

PDFescape

Need to edit a PDF file? PDFescape is a free online program that provides users with the ability to edit PDF files, view PDF files, create new PDF forms, annotate PDF documents, password protect PDF files, and fill out PDF forms. Typically, paid software is needed to create PDF documents; yet PDFescapes offers all of the same services for free with no downloads necessary. In addition to filling in a PDF forms, the program gives users the ability to edit existing text and images.

A few of the interesting features of PDFescapes:

- PDF pages can be rotated and zoomed
- Text can be copied to a clipboard
- PDF documents can be opened in a web browser
- Text and shapes can be added to PDF files
- Pages can be cropped, moved, or deleted
- A scanned signature can be used to sign PDF documents
- New form fields can be easily added
- Ability to strike out existing text
- Ability to merge multiple PDF files
- Option to insert watermarks and page numbers
- Confidential content can be permanently blacked out

Whether you need to make changes to a current PDF form, create a new one, or publish a form for others to fill out, PDFescape is a great free resource.

Website: https://www.pdfescape.com

Google Docs, Sheets, and Slides

Using a Google account and Google Drive, users can create Docs, Sheets, and Slides as an alternative to Word documents, Excel spreadsheets, and PowerPoint slides, respectively. With the ability to easily share with other Google users, allowing multiple users to edit and add to documents, Google Drive apps have become increasingly popular in the business world.

Google Docs

Google Docs allow you to do basically everything that other word processor programs do, including formatting documents, changing fonts and colors, adding spacing, and adjusting margins. Anyone with access to the document (through the sharing capabilities) can comment, view, and edit the document. Word documents can easily be uploaded and converted into a Google Doc. Emailing documents is incredibly easy with Google Docs.

Google Sheets

Google Sheets provides users with the ability to format spreadsheets and share them with others. Excel, .txt, .csv, and .ods files can all be converted into a Google Sheet. Like other spreadsheet programs, Google Sheets gives users the option of creating charts and using formulas to calculate the data that is entered.

Google Slides

This presentation app provides an avenue for creating and sharing work that is best displayed using visual slides. Google users can create presentations and share them with coworkers so that a team can edit and work on a project using this cloud-based technology. Images and videos can be added to presentations and Google Slides can be embedded into a website.

Website: https://www.google.com/docs/about/

Google Drive

Google Drive provides Google users with the ability to store files in the cloud, allowing access from any device, anywhere. With Google Drive, gone are the days of storing and backing up files on a personal computer. A free Google Drive account automatically includes 15 GB of storage and more storage can be purchased. Through Google Drive, users can save photos and use Googles Apps to create files using Google Docs, Google Sheets, and Google Slides. Files can be added from a personal or business computer using the upload option.

Google Drive allows file sharing, which comes in handy if two or more people are working on a business project together. Shared files can be viewed or edited by those with access. Files can be renamed, deleted, or moved at the user's discretion and can be sorted using folders for easy access. Important files can be starred.

Dropbox

Dropbox provides a way to upload any file and then access it from any device. A Dropbox account is synced to all user devices. Users can upload photos, music, videos, adobe files, Microsoft office files, and others. It does not matter whether users use a Mac, iPad, iPhone, Android, PC, or Windows phone – Dropbox has been designed to work with all devices.

Benefits of Dropbox:

Dropbox makes sharing large files such as videos much simpler and quicker than other options. A link to large files can be shared with friends and coworkers via email, text message, or chat. Recipients do not have to have a Dropbox account.

Photos can be backed up from phone or computer, so that they are safe and secure. They can then be accessed from any device via Dropbox account.

Dropbox offers users the option to share files and folders so that multiple people can add to and edit a project without the hassle of having to email files back and forth. Updates are sent automatically.

Even if a user loses their phone, computer, or other device, all files and photos on Dropbox are protected.

Files can be accessed offline so that work does not need to stop when there is no connection.

Website: https://www.dropbox.com/

Evernote

Evernote takes note taking to a whole new level. Evernote is for individuals who need a bit of help staying organized. Using Evernote, users can take notes, snap pictures of handwritten notes to keep track of, take a picture of a sketch or drawing, or create a to-do list. Notes are instantly saved and accessible from any device.

Evernote offers four membership tiers, ranging in price from free to $120 per year. The basic (free) membership allows users to track tasks, take notes, "clip" important things found online, share and discuss, and sync user devices. The plus membership, at $24.99 per year, adds the ability to access notes offline, save emails, and add a passcode lock.

Website: https://www.evernote.com/

WOULD YOU LIKE TO
KNOW MORE?

I'm glad that you enjoyed this power-packed resource guide. It was a labor of love that I birthed and am happy to bring to you.

I would be happy to connect with you on social media so that you can share your story of how this book has impacted your life.

If you want to receive even more in-depth content or just ask me questions about my journey or some other related topic, send me an email. Ask to be added to the list of my email subscribers. I will only be sending out relevant content based on feedback from readers.

Feel free to connect with me on LinkedIn, Instagram, or follow me on Twitter.

You can join me on any of my upcoming webinars discussing federal contracting. All of that information will be sent out to my list of email subscribers.

ADDITIONAL FREE OFFERS

For tons of free resources, videos, interviews with successful government contractors and federal officers, head over to www.govcongiants.com/resources

DID YOU LIKE *BILLION-DOLLAR PLAYBOOK*?

If you liked the book please go to Amazon and share your feedback. I would greatly appreciate it.

Made in the USA
Monee, IL
10 August 2022

11335792R00059